112 Gripes about the French

1945

Dear Henry,
think of the French as
Momentum and see if this
helps.

love
Tom

Bodleian Library
UNIVERSITY OF OXFORD

First published in 1945 by the Information & Education Division of the US Occupation Forces, Paris.

This edition first published in 2013 by the Bodleian Library
Broad Street
Oxford OX1 3BG

www.bodleianbookshop.co.uk

Reprinted in 2014

ISBN: 978 1 85124 039 5

This edition © Bodleian Library, University of Oxford, 2013.

Cover design adapted from original by Dot Little
Designed and typeset by JCS Publishing Services Ltd
in 9.75 on 11.75 Century Schoolbook

Printed and bound in China by C&C Offset Printing Co. Ltd on 100gsm SenPo Endlanda paper

British Library Catalogue in Publishing Data
A CIP record of this publication is available from the British Library

CONTENTS

INTRODUCTION

While Charles de Gaulle marched his troops down the Champs-Élysées on 26 August 1944 to drive home the fact that Paris had been liberated by the French, he nevertheless needed the help of the American army in maintaining law and order in France, then and for a period after liberation. The sheer number of American GIs involved is worth recalling. 'When the invasion of Normandy was launched on June 6th, 1944, more than 1.5 million US Army personnel were on hand . . . At the end of the war, the total US Army strength in Europe was almost 1.9 million.'*

At first, the smart, well-dressed American soldiers were received by the French populace with a sense of euphoria. However, the mind-set of these foreign 'guests' did not endear them to their hosts for long. The idea that the French were collaborators, little better than the German or Japanese foe, was not an uncommon attitude among American GIs. The Americans had long recognized solely the Vichy government as the legitimate government of France and only finally acknowledged the reality on the ground on 11 July 1944 by grudgingly granting the Free French the status of a working *de facto* authority in French civil affairs in liberated areas, until elections could be held. The main aim

---

* US Army Europe: the official homepage of the United States Army in Europe http://www.eur.army.mil/organization/history.htm.

iv

of the Americans was to defeat Nazi Germany; French interests were subordinate to that.

As the reality of post-liberation daily life set in, the affection of the local populace for their liberators continued to wane. There were food shortages and difficulties in obtaining basic supplies. The French resented the Americans for their brash behaviour and their relative wealth. Moreover, it has emerged in recent years just how widespread rape, violence and the use of prostitutes by the American forces were. The Americans, on the other hand, found the French proud and resentful, their habits and customs difficult to understand.

A fear developed among the officials of a rapid deterioration in relations between the French and the American GIs. Something had to be done. The American generals responded by commissioning a book which sought to address directly the soldiers' most common complaints about the locals and crucially to change the way in which they viewed them. This book is divided into sections consisting of questions and answers, the kind of questions that the ordinary American GI might come up with. Collectively these questions and answers offer a fascinating insight into the situation immediately after liberation, describing in highly evocative terms the shortage of supplies, the high prices charged to American GIs, the black market, the destruction of property, accusations of collaboration during the war and the low morale of the French.

Yet many of the complaints have a perennial quality: 'The French are cynical', 'The French are unsanitary', 'Why do they knock off work for two to three hours every day?', 'The French spend all their time at these cafés. They just sit around drinking instead of working', 'French women are immoral', 'The French drink too much', 'The French drive like lunatics! They don't obey traffic laws, they don't even use common sense.'

One finds oneself looking for one's own gripes and not always finding them; there is nothing, for instance, about the French signposting of roads that is often so mystifying to drivers from other countries, nothing said about the French system of *priorité à droite*, French loos, certain French dishes . . . Until the last decades of the twentieth century and the relentless onset of globalization, France was indeed a very different country to the USA (and arguably still is).

Sometimes the remarks about the Germans risk creating another stereotype: 'The Germans obey the law – even if the laws are barbaric laws' seems to be something of an over-simplification. There are a few factual inaccuracies too: Madame de Curie ('What did these frogs ever contribute to the world anyway?') was surely Polish by birth. Some of the gripes are frankly surprising or even incredible – knowing what we know now, it is hard to believe that many American GIs complained about the immorality of the local women. Some of the explanations are slightly puzzling, if not risible. Is it really true that the Germans 'took the soap, for four years' ('The French don't bathe')?

What does come across strongly, however, is that the anonymous author(s) of this book are Francophiles. Their praise for France, the French way of life, their sufferings during the war and their subsequent plight is unstinting.

FOREWORD

*Americans believe in the right to criticize. We
defend out right to "beef" or "gripe" or "sound
off". We insist upon the right to express our own
opinions.*

*But we also believe in the right of others to
express their opinions. For the right to speak
involves the duty to listen. The right to criticize
involves the responsibility of giving "the other side"
a fair chance to make its point. We know that the
truth can only be found through open and honest
discussion, and that the common good is served
through common attempts to reach common under-
standing. In one way, Democracy is the long and
sometimes difficult effort which free men make to
understand each other.*

*The booklet tries to help some of us understand
an ally —the French. It is not meant either to
"defend" the French or to chastise those Americans
who do not like the French. It is intended simply to
bring into reasonable focus those irritations, dis-
satisfactions and misunderstandings which arise
because it is often hard for the people of one country
to understand the people of another.*

*The booklet uses the Question–Answer form.
It lists the criticisms, misconceptions and ordinary "gripes" which American troops in Europe
express most frequently when they talk about the
French. Each comment, or question, is followed by*

an answer—or discussion. Some of the answers are quite short, because the question is direct and simple. Some of the answers are quite long, because the "questions" are not questions at all, but indictments which contain complicated and sweeping preconceptions.

The purpose of the present publication is this: to present facts and judgments which even the well-intentioned may tend to overlook.

There may be those who will consider this booklet a catalogue of "excuses" or "justifications". To them it can only be said that the truth is not denied by giving it a derogatory label.

There may be others who will seize upon the questions with triumph—ignoring the discussions entirely. That kind of reader will ignore the truth anyway—in whatever form it is offered.

This booklet may not convince those who are hopelessly prejudiced, but it may help to keep others from being infected by the same lamentable virus.

the French

AND US

I *"We came to Europe twice in twenty-five years to save the French."*

We didn't come to Europe to save the French, either in 1917 or in 1944. We didn't come to Europe to do anyone any favors. We came to Europe because we in America were threatened by a hostile, aggressive and very dangerous power.

In this war, France fell in June of 1940. We didn't invade Europe until June of 1944. We didn't even think of "saving the French" through military action until after Pearl Harbor—after the Germans declared war on us.

We came to Europe, in two wars, because it was better to fight our enemy in Europe than in America. Would it have been smarter to fight the Battle of the Bulge in Ohio? Would it have been smarter if D-Day had meant a hop across the Atlantic Ocean, instead of the English Channel, in order to get at an enemy sending rocket bombs crashing into our homes? Would it have been smart to wait in America until V bombs, buzz bombs, rocket bombs, and—perhaps—atomic bombs had made shambles of our cities? Even the kids in Germany sang this song: "Today Germany, tomorrow the world." We were a part of that world. We were marked for conquest.

When France fell, *our* last defense on the Continent was gone. France was the "keystone of freedom" on land from the Mediterranean to the North Sea; it was a bulwark against German aggression. France guarded the Atlantic, and the bases the Germans needed on the Atlantic for submarine and air warfare.

American security and American foreign policy have always rested on this hard fact: we cannot permit a hostile power on the Atlantic Ocean. We cannot be secure if we are threatened on the Atlantic. That's why we went to war in 1917; that's why we had to fight in 1944. And that's why, as a matter of common sense and the national interest, President Roosevelt declared (November 11, 1941): "The defense of any territory under the control of the French Volunteer Forces (the Free French) is vital to the defense of the United States."

2 *"At first, when we came into Normandy, and then into Paris, the French gave us everything—wine, cheese, fruit, everything. They threw their arms around us and kissed us every time we turned around. They gave us the biggest welcome you ever saw. But they've forgotten. They're ungrateful."*

Perhaps the French ran out of wine, cheese, fruit and cognac to pass out free. Perhaps the French depleted the stocks they had hidden in their cellars from the Germans.

Could not a Frenchman who read the question above ask, "Are the Americans so ungrateful? Have they so soon forgotten how much we gave them from what little we had?"

3

3 *"The French don't invite us into their homes."*

They don't have the food. (The Germans took it.)

They don't speak English and we don't speak French. It's hard to extend hospitality under those conditions.

Ask those soldiers who *have* been invited into a French home what it was like.

How many American homes were you invited into when you were stationed near a "soldier town" in the States?

4 *"The French rub me the wrong way."*

It was inevitable that some Frenchmen would rub some Americans the wrong way. City people often rub country folk the wrong way; the same goes for a Pittsburgher in New Orleans, or a Texan on Fifth Avenue.

We Americans believe in the value of differences—*if* basic political beliefs and goals rest on a common foundation. (See question § 69.)

"Unless you bear with the faults of a friend you betray your own."

5 *"I'll never love the French."*
   "I hate the French!"

You don't have to love the French. You don't have to hate them either. You might try to understand them.

The more important point is not to let your feeling blind you to the fact that they were and are our *allies*. They were in 1917, too.

The most important question any people can ask itself is this: "Who fights with us? Who fights against us?"

6 *"We're always pulling the French out of a jam. Did they ever do anything for us?"*

They did. They helped us out of one of the greatest jams we were ever in. During the American Revolution, when almost the entire world stood by in "non intervention" or was against us, it was France who was our greatest ally and benefactor. France loaned the thirteen states $6,000,000—and *gave* us over $3,000,000 more. (That was a lot more money in those days than it is now.)

45,000 Frenchmen volunteered in the army of George Washington. They crossed the Atlantic Ocean in small boats that took two months to make the voyage.

Washington's army had no military engineers; it was French engineers who designed and built our fortifications.

The name of Lafayette is one that Americans will never forget, and the French are as proud of that name as we are.

You can judge the measure and meaning of French aid to our Revolution from the letter George Washington sent on April 9, 1781 to our military envoy in Paris, asking for help from France:

"We are at this hour suspended in the balance; not from choice but from hard and absolute necessity . . . Our troops are fast approaching nakedness . . . our hospitals are without medicines and our sick without nutrition . . . in a word, we are at the end of our tether, and . . . now or never our deliverance must come."

It was France that came to our aid in our darkest hour.

7 *"We can't rely on these French."*

That depends on what you mean by "rely". If you expect the French to react like Americans, you will be disappointed. They are not Americans; they are French. If you expect the French to hurry the way we do, you will be disappointed; the French don't hurry—neither do most of the people in the world outside of America.

But we *were* able to rely on the French for the most important thing: France fought with us, not against us, twice in the past two decades.

8 *"We've had more beefing from the French than from the Germans. We are always quarreling with them. They criticize everything. They have to put their two cents in. But the Germans— they just do what you tell them to. They're co-operative; the French aren't."*

Two men working together are more likely to tell each other off than a prisoner is to tell off the warden.

Of course we differ with the French; of course we argue with them. Why? Because we have a common goal and face common problems. Because we, like the French, have been taught to think for ourselves, to "put our two cents in". Democracy is based on the idea that everyone has a basic right to "put his two cents in". In America we say, "I'm from Missouri" or "Sez who?" The French have the same attitude; they say, *"Je ne crois que ce que je vois."* ("I only believe what I see.") Or *"Je ne demande pas mieux que d'être convaincu."* ("I don't ask much; I just want to be convinced.")

There is a saying that in France everything is permitted that is not strictly forbidden—but in Germany everything is *verboten* that is not strictly permitted. We are in the French, not the German, tradition.

Yes, we quarrel with the French. The members of a family argue pretty freely inside the home. We quarrel with our *allies*. We don't quarrel with our enemies—we fight them.

As for the Germans, they've *got* to be "co-operative". They have no choice. They're under military law.

Which is better: a critical ally or a fawning enemy?

"Flatterers are the worst kind of enemies."
—Tacitus.

9 *"We gave the French uniforms, jeeps, trucks, supplies, ammunition—everything."*

We didn't *give* the French these things. We *lent* them, under Lend-Lease, a law passed by our Congress as "An Act to Promote the Defense of the United States". We lent military equipment and supplies to our *ally*.

Where else could the French have gotten uniforms, guns, ammunition, supplies? From the Germans?

A Frenchman armed with an 03 rifle could kill Germans. It was wiser for us to turn out weapons and uniforms to arm the French than to turn out additional American soldiers.

10 *"We gave the French billions of dollars worth of stuff. They'll never pay it back."*

Under Lend-Lease we provided military supplies and equipment to France worth $1,041,000,000.

Under reverse Lend-Lease, the French have already paid back about $450,000,000—almost half of the amount we lent them in the way of military supplies.

The French paid this $450,000,000 back in the same way that they got it from us—with supplies, materials, food, labor, services.

Here are some of the things the French have provided us:

131,000 snow capes for the winter campaign of 1944.

700 tons of rubber tires, made in France.

260,000 signs and posters for road markers during the military campaign.

Millions of jerricans.

150,000 French workmen and civilians, working for the United States Army and paid by the French government. These French men and women work at airfields, railway yards, ports, docks, in offices, etc. They range from stevedores to nurses, mechanics to typists, in France, North Africa, and the French islands in the South Pacific, such as New Caledonia, where American troops are stationed.

All French telephone and telegraph services were placed at our disposal.

Lumber, cement, gravel for construction purposes.

Billets—all through France, from Brest to Strasbourg, from Paris to Nice or Biarritz.

Theaters such as the Olympia, the Empire, the Marignan in Paris.

Restaurants—for American mess halls.

Food—though the French are very short of it themselves. The French supply us with such fresh fruit and vegetables as can be spared.

Beer—made in France, by the French, for American troops, from ingredients shipped from the United States.

Printing—Stars and Stripes, Yank, Army Talks, Overseas Woman, I and E pamphlets.

11 *"The French are using our gas, but they won't give it to Americans. You can't get gas in the French zones of occupation if you're driving through."*

You are not supposed to.

The French are given gasoline by U.S. Army authority. It is the only gasoline they get. They are compelled to use it for themselves.

The Reciprocal Aid Agreement, under Lend-Lease laws, states (Article III) that the Government of France will not, without the consent of the President of the U.S., transfer any articles provided the French, or permit their use, by anyone not an officer, employee, or agent of the French government.

Can an American gas pump give gasoline to a French army car which is not specifically authorized to obtain gasoline from an American pump? If you were on duty would you give gasoline to unauthorized persons?

12 *"One Frenchman told me the French practically gave us the Statue of Liberty. How do you like that?"*

The Statue of Liberty began as the idea of a group of Frenchmen, shortly after the Civil War. They commissioned a French sculptor, Frederic Auguste Bartholdi, to do the work. A committee of Frenchmen was formed in 1874 to raise funds.

Bartholdi recommended the site for the statue—
Bedloe's Island in New York harbor.

In France, 180 French cities, forty general
councils, and thousands of anonymous Frenchmen contributed a quarter of a million dollars (not
francs) towards the statue. (The United States
raised $280,000.) In 1883, the President of the
French Committee, Mr. de Lesseps, officially pre-
sented the statue to the American people.

13 *"We are not welcome in French restaurants."*

Why should we be? We are supposed to eat in
army messes. Every meal we might eat in a French
restaurant would use up just that much food from
the Frenchmen's limited supply.

14 *"Every time we go into a night club, we get
soaked by these Frenchmen"*

Were you never soaked in a night club at home?
Compare the prices in Paris night clubs to those
in the night clubs you've visited in Miami or New
York, Chicago or Los Angeles.

A GI comes out of a night club in the States and
says, "A buck and half for a Scotch and soda! That
place is a clip joint!" The same GI comes out of a
night club in Paris and says, "Ninety francs for a
shot of cognac! That's the French for you—they're
all robbers!"

15 *"The French are terrible scroungers. They keep mooching candy, soap, cigarettes, food from the GIs. They have no self-respect."*

Some of the French are scroungers.

Hungry people lose their pride.

An empty stomach does not worry about losing face.

16 *"The French welcomed as at first; now they want us to get out."*

An American GI recently said, "We're like people who were given a wonderful reception for a week-end. But we've stayed in the house for a year. No one wants a house guest that long."

Of course the French would prefer that American troops leave France as soon as possible. (So would you, if you were a Frenchman.) As long as we are here, we impose an added strain on the already overtaxed French economy. The French need the billets and food and supplies and services which they are now supplying to us.

(See question § 10.)

17 *"The French brag a lot about the fighting they did, but you don't hear any Americans passing out bouquets to them."*

General Patton cabled General Koenig, the French commander of the FFI, that the spectacular advance of his (Patton's) army across France would have been impossible without the fighting aid of the FFI.

General Patch estimated that from the time of the Mediterranean landings to the arrival of our troops at Dijon, the help given to our operations by the FFI was equivalent to four full divisions.

The Maquis who defended the Massif Central, in the south-central part of France, had two Nazi divisions stymied; they kept those two divisions from fighting against us.

The magnificent fight the Free French put up at Bir Hakeim, in the Libyan campaign, will be long remembered in the annals of heroism.

Perhaps some of us don't like to pass out bouquets—to anyone but ourselves. Perhaps we have short memories.

18 *"The French let us down when the fighting got tough. What did they do—as fighters—to help us out?"*

Here are a few of the things the French did:

The French fought in Africa, in Sicily, liberated Corsica, fought in Italy, took part in the invasion of Europe and fought through the battles of France and Germany—from Normandy to Munich.

Units from the French navy participated in the invasions of Sicily, Italy, Normandy and South France.

Units of the French navy and merchant marine

took part in convoying operations on the Atlantic and Murmansk routes.

On June 5, 1944, the day before D-Day, over 5,000 Frenchmen of the resistance dynamited railroads in more than 500 strategic places.

They delayed strategic German troop movements for an average of 48 hours, according to our military experts. Those 48 hours were tactically priceless; they saved an untold number of American lives.

French resistance groups blew up a series of bridges in southern France and delayed one of the Wehrmacht's crack units (Das Reich Panzer Division) for *twelve days* in getting from Bordeaux to Normandy.

About 30,000 FFI troops supported the Third Army's VIII Corps in Brittany: they seized and held key spots; they conducted extensive guerrilla operations behind the German lines.

25,000 FFI troops protected the south flank of the Third Army in its daring dash across France: the FFI wiped out German bridgeheads north of the Loire River; they guarded vital lines of communication; they wiped out pockets of German resistance; they held many towns and cities under orders from our command.

When our Third Army was approaching the area between Dijon and Troyes from the west, and while the Seventh Army was approaching this sector from the south, it was the FFI who stubbornly blocked the Germans from making a stand and prevented a mass retirement of German troops.

In Paris, as our armies drew close, several hundred thousand French men and women rose up against the Germans. 50,000 armed men of the resistance fought and beat the Nazi garrison, and occupied the main buildings and administrative offices of Paris.

These are some of the things the French did. For others, see question § 104.

19 *"They ride in our jeeps and waste our gas."*

They ride in the jeeps which are officially loaned to them by our government.

How do you know they are wasting gas? How do you know their trips are not on official business? Did no Americans waste gas on pleasure trips?

20 *"The French aren't friendly."*

Some Frenchmen are; other Frenchmen are not.

The French as a whole are not as "hail fellow well met" as we Americans are. Neither are the British, the Swedes, the Greeks, the Mexicans.

Frenchmen don't get personal or confidential quickly. They don't "open up" as quickly as we do in the States. The French are very polite; they are also more formal than we are about personal relationships. (So are the Chinese.) The French respect another person's privacy, and they like to have their own privacy respected too.

It is natural for anyone to think the people of another nation are not as friendly as his own people. It's hard to be friendly in a foreign language. It's hard to be friendly when you're hungry, cold, and have gone through six years of war—as the French have. Yet the Americans who came into Normandy, or who came into Paris right after the liberation, still talk about the astonishing outburst of gratitude, generosity and friendliness which the French displayed toward us.

Back in the States, many of our troops complained that the people in the towns near the training camps were not friendly. People from our South often complain that the people in the North are not friendly. A Texan in Vermont finds New Englanders "cold" and "snobbish". Do we then say that all Americans are unfriendly?

Friendship, said a wise man, lies in this: "To desire the same things and to reject the same things." On this basis, the United States has never had a better friend than France. (See question § 69.)

21 *"Why bother about the French? They won't throw any weight in the post-war world."*

Apart from reasons of honor and simple decency (Americans are not in the habit of letting their friends down), it is poor politics and worse diplomacy to "write off" a nation of 40 million allies. You may need their help some day.

France still stands as a bastion on the Atlantic, from the Mediterranean to the North Sea. France will still be a strong factor in world political organization. The island bases of France, and her colonies, will still be strategic areas in the world structure of peace. And in the age of the atomic bomb, the physical size and population of a country may be no index of her strength and potentialities.

Why bother about France? It is not our job to "bother about" France. But it *is* our job to be seriously concerned about the peace and the political problems of the world. France is very much a part of that world.

David Low, the English cartoonist, once drew a famous cartoon showing the nations in a large rowboat. The European nations were at one end of the boat, which was foundering in the water; Uncle Sam sat in the other end, high and dry and out of the water. And Uncle Sam was saying, "Why should I worry? The leak isn't in my end of the boat!" We have paid a terrible price for believing that a leak "at the other end of the boat" does not affect our destiny.

the French

A. *CHARACTERISTICS*

B. *CUSTOMS AND MANNERS*

C. *CLEANLINESS AND SANITATION*

D. *WORK AND LAZINESS*

E. *MORALS*

F. *AUTOMOBILES AND LOCOMOTIVES*

A. CHARACTERISTICS

22 *"The French are too damned independent."*

The French *are* independent. They are proud. They are individualists. So are we. That's one reason there is friction between us.

23 *"The French are out for what they can get. They always play the winner."*

They didn't in 1939, when it looked to all the world as though the Germans were sure winners. The French and British could have let the Germans rape Poland without a protest. The French and British declared war on Germany.

Most of the French didn't play the winner in 1940 either, when it looked even more that Germany was unbeatable. While some of their leaders in the Vichy government played ball with the Germans, the vast majority of the people refused to; they resisted in whatever way they could.

24 *"The French are mercenary. They'll do anything for a couple of hundred francs."*

Where do you draw the line between a "smart businessman" and a "mercenary Frenchman?"

The French think that the American soldier who sells cigarettes, soap or candy on the black market at fantastic prices is mercenary. Some

Americans will "do anything for a couple of hundred francs".

25 *"The French are gypping us."*

Some Frenchmen have certainly gypped *some* Americans.

We remember the times we were gypped. We forget the number of times we were not. How many times were you treated fairly, honestly?

Were you never "gypped" back home—in towns near army camps? (See question § 85).

26 *"The French are cynical."*

The French are disillusioned. They are bitter. They have a right to be. They have gone through six of the most disastrous years of history. They have experienced defeat, hunger, persecution, invasion, occupation, despair. They have been humiliated before the eyes of the world.

The cynical comments which many of us have heard in France are a reflection of the profound shock and confusion the French have suffered for the past six years.

Cynical talk, by the way, is often considered "smart" and "sophisticated"—in the United States no less than in France. We Americans love to give the "low down"; we love to tell "the inside story". So do the French.

But the French are not cynical about certain

21

things, about ideas like "Liberty, Equality, Fraternity". They mean it. They have always fought for it.

27 *"The French are not up-to-date. They're not modern. They're living in the past."*

Change comes slowly in France. On the whole, the French are conservative. If the average Frenchman has a secure living, he is satisfied. His dream is not to become a millionaire, but to retire on a "little" fortune so that he can have a "little" home and a "little" garden and read his paper.

The French are certainly not highly industrialized as we are. Compared to some other nations, however, they are considered very up-to-date. It depends on what standard you use. The French are as far advanced as any nation in the world today in some fields: art, literature, music, design, silk manufacture, textiles, etc.

The World Almanac for 1945 concludes that as far as social legislation is concerned, "France is in the vanguard". The French were certainly up-to-date in establishing old age pensions, compulsory insurance against illness, disability and death, maternity insurance, and so on. It was France that introduced the forty-hour work week.

28 *"The French won't accept new ideas. They're not inventive."*

Here are some of the inventions and discoveries which have come from France:

Aluminium (discovered simultaneously in U.S. and France)

Braille system of reading for the blind

Breech-loading shotgun

Cellophane

Commercial gas engine

Electric steel

Electric storage battery

Flying balloon

Gyroscope

Iron galvanizing process

Laminated glass

Machine for making paper

Metallic cartridge

Pasteurization

Phosphorus match

Photography

Rayon

Rayon nitrocellulose

Screw propeller

Sewing machine

Smokeless powder

Steam automobile

Steam pressure gauge

Stethoscope

Synthesis of camphor

Television 1000 line screen

The Nobel Prize has been awarded since 1901 for contributions in Physics, Chemistry, Medicine and Physiology, Literature and the Advancement of Peace. The prizes are awarded irrespective of nationality, race or creed. From 1901 to 1939, the Nobel Prize has been awarded to 203 individuals. The United States won 25. The French won 28.

The only person who has ever been awarded the Nobel Prize twice was Mme Marie Curie.

29 *"The French are always criticizing. Nothing is right; everything has something wrong with it."*

That sounds as though the French are like us. We Americans are always griping about something. We're never satisfied. We criticize our allies, our government, our army, our police, our politicians, our business leaders, our union leaders, our schools, our taxes, etc., etc. We are very proud of our right to criticize.

As people in a democracy, we demand the right to criticize whatever we want, at any time, on any issue.

The French, too, have a very strong individualistic, democratic tradition. Beware the people who do not criticize. Beware the country where criticism is *verboten*. Beware the country where men obey like sheep.

30 *"All the French want is a good time. That's all they think about in Paris."*

If you judge the French by those you see on the Champs Elysees or in Montmartre, you are making the same mistake that was made by the tourist who visited the House of David and asked "Why don't Americans shave?"

Paris is not France, any more than 52nd Street is America. Paris has for several hundred years been one of the great tourist attractions of the world.

As a matter of fact, the French have much *less* of the "having a good time" habit than we do. The average French family ordinarily spends less on pleasure in a month than we do on a week-end.

The French reputation for gaiety was built on the fame of Paris as a gay city and on the French way of doing things. The French theater was always bright and varied. Paris' cabarets and music halls were famed throughout the world. But there are about 35 million Frenchmen who do not live in Paris.

31 *"The French are insincere; it is an inborn trait with them."*

There are no "inborn traits" which account for the social characteristics or customs of a people. The entire body of scientific anthropology proves this.

A French child, of French descent, will react like an American if that child is raised in an American home in an American town. The same goes for a child of any other nationality, color or creed.

To talk about "inborn traits" is talk just as the Nazis did when they talked about "good" or "bad" blood. It just does not jibe with fact or science.

To say that the French are insincere is no more sensible than to say that Bostonians have an "inborn trait" for baked beans, or that Brooklynites have an "inborn trait" for throwing pop bottles at the umpire.

Are the French "insincere"? The way to answer this intelligently is to define insincerity, analyze the number of Frenchmen who show these characteristics, compare this number to the number of Frenchmen who do *not* show these characteristics, get the relative proportions between the two groups, then compare the proportions to a similar analysis of the "insincerity" of other nations, including the Papuans.

32 *"The French just don't care about anything. They've even got a phrase for it—laissez-faire. That means why bother? Just let everything alone!"*

"Laissez-faire" is the name for a philosophy of economics. It means "let alone"—let the economy run by itself, by the laws of supply and demand, without governmental interference or protection.

The whole system we call capitalism, or free enterprise, rests on the idea of laissez-faire.

33 *"The French have no guts; they're decadent."*

From the editorial columns of the *New York Times* at the time France fell:

"The reporters of the exodus of the French pay tribute to the courage, the patience, the dauntless spirit of the people on the roads. They all agree that the peasant refugee preserves under a terrible ordeal his characteristic faith in himself and his country. The peasant is France, steady, tough, independent and brave . . . Nobody who knows the grass roots of France can doubt that even under Nazi occupation the Republic will survive, will be reincarnated, may in the long run be the force which will help to fashion the Fourth Republic."

34 *"What did these frogs ever contribute to the world anyway?"*

Apart from the fact that the basic conceptions of freedom, liberty, human rights, and government by the people received their greatest impetus from the French writers and thinkers of the period called the Enlightenment, "these frogs" have made contributions to history, literature, science, art, philosophy and political ideas which make one of the proudest and most brilliant records in the civilization of mankind.

The record of France can stand beside that of any other nation in the world, and in many fields stands well above any other nation. Here are some

of the French names which any literate person
regards with respect:

Writers

Villon	Mérimée	Jules Verne
Rabelais	Prévost	Mme de Staël
Corneille	Ronsard	Stendhal
La Fontaine	Sardou	Gautier
Molière	Le Sage	de Goncourt
Racine	Verlaine	Lamartine
Voltaire	Flaubert	Sue
Rousseau	Zola	Loti
Balzac	de Maupassant	Mme de Sévigné
Victor Hugo	Anatole France	Proust
Dumas	Daudet	Jules Romains
Georges Sand	Romain Rolland	André Malraux
de Musset	Rostand	

Explorers

Cartier	La Salle	Marquette
Champlain		

Scientists and Inventors

Pascal	Laennec	Toucanta
Pasteur	Cuvier	Bourdon
Curie	Levassor	Chardonnet
Buffon	Braille	Heroult
Berthelot	Haller	Sauvage
Ampère	Lavoisier	Sauria
Daguerre	Montgolfier	Le Blanc

Musicians

Bizet	Saint Saëns	Debussy
Gounod	Massenet	Lalo
Berlioz	Favre	Ravel

Painters and Sculptors

Cezanne	Houdon	Prudhon
Corot	Ingres	Renoir
Degas	Lebrun	Rodin
Delacroix	Matisse	Rousseau, P. E. T.
David	Meissonier	Rouault
Doré	Millet	Toulouse-Lautrec
Forain	Poussin	Seurat
Gerôme		

Philosophers

Chateaubriand	Condorcet	Comte
Charron	Cousin	Bergson
Calvin	Rousseau	Maritain
Montesquieu	Descartes	Poincaré
Abelard	Montaigne	Rochefoucauld
La Bruyère	Pascal	Renan
Diderot		

Historians

de Tocqueville	Taine	Saint-Simon
Guizot	Thierry	Quinet
Thiers		

B. CUSTOMS AND MANNERS

35 *"The French do things different than we do. That's what I don't like."*

It is always something of a shock when you run into different ways of talking, eating, doing things. But what is different is not always inferior: "different" does not mean "worse". There is more than one way of skinning a cat.

The story is told of an American soldier who saw some Chinese putting rice on the graves in a Chungking cemetery. "That doesn't make sense", said the American with a smile. "When do you expect the dead to eat the rice?"

"When your dead return to smell your flowers", was the answer.

36 *"All the French do is talk."*

No nation could exist for a week if all it did was talk.

Frenchmen enjoy conversation. They consider it an art. They are on the whole, skillful at it.

We don't prize "good conversation" as much as the French do.

It was the brilliance, charm and imagination of French talk that contributed much to the reputation of Paris as a world center of gaiety.

37 *"I never heard people gab so much. Gab, gab, gab."*

If you understood the language it might be interesting and not just "gab".

An American writer, Ambrose Bierce, said, "A bore is a person who talks—when you want him to listen."

38 *"Why do Frenchmen look so shabby?"*

Because they are wearing pre-war clothes—clothes that are five and six years old. New clothes are for the most part reserved for repatriated French PWs and deportees.

The average Frenchman never looked as well dressed as the average American. The average Frenchman had a lot less money than the average American.

39 *"What amazes me is how, with all their stories about suffering, you see so many well-dressed Frenchmen."*

The places we frequent in Paris are comparable to the rich or "touristy" neighborhoods of any big American city—Fifth Avenue, Michigan Boulevard, Wilshire Boulevard. It is on the Champs Elysees, around l'Opera and on the Boulevard Haussman that you see *those* Frenchmen who are well-dressed. It is there, too, that you see those who profit from the inflation and the black market.

Some of the Frenchmen who look so well dressed are well dressed only in the places you see. Under a good collar and cuffs, there may be the oldest, most patched-up shirt you ever saw. Socks are made of pieces of old cloth. Underwear is made of anything a person can lay his hands on.

40 *"Why do the French parade all the time? Take the Champs Elysees, for example; every time you turn around there is a parade."*

They don't parade all the time. They do parade more than we do. They have more holidays. They have had a much longer and more complicated history. Since 1789, France has had two empires, two monarchies, and three republics.

In France, as in America, there are a great many organizations (like our American Legion, VFWs, Masons, Odd Fellows, etc.) which hold annual meetings or conventions or parades.

In France, as in any country which has been liberated after being under the heel of a conqueror for four years, there is an understandable upsurge of patriotism—and a desire to celebrate liberation, to honor their martyrs, to commemorate their resistance.

41 *"At the Folies Bergere or the Casino de Paris, even the usher girls demand tips! What a racket!"*

It isn't a racket. We don't think that tipping taxi-drivers, waitresses or red caps is a "racket".

In some theaters in France, the ushers pay for their job (like our check-room concessions). In most theaters the ushers get little or no salary and depend for their livelihood on tips. Frenchmen always tip ushers at movie houses, theaters, the Opera, symphony halls. The usher who serves a dozen Americans who do not tip has lost the money which a dozen Frenchmen would have given her.

C. CLEANLINESS AND SANITATION

42 *"Why isn't there decent plumbing in French houses? The toilet facilities are disgraceful!"*

They are. What should the French do about it? It takes money to have decent plumbing. That's why so many people in France don't have it. That's why so many people in our own United States don't have decent plumbing either.

The Germans have much better plumbing than the French—the Germans could afford it.

Most French buildings are very old: it's harder and more expensive to install plumbing in an old house than in a new one.

Incidentally, 9,400,000 homes in the U.S. do not have electricity. 80% of the farmhouses do not have bathrooms and running water. About

3,607,724 homes do not have private flushing toilets.

43 *"French cities are filthy."*

They are certainly dirtier today than they were before the war. The French haven't had paint for a long time.

In some cities and districts, the acute shortage of gasoline prevents refuse trucks from making daily rounds.

French cities and houses are a great deal older than ours; old cities and old houses smell more than new ones.

French public sanitation, health and toilet regulations are certainly not on the same level as ours.

But before the war, the French washed their streets and sidewalks more often than we do. France does not have the untidy back yards, the trash dumps in empty lots, the tin cans and refuse in public parks that are common in the United States.

French women were always scrupulous housekeepers. But few of us ever got in to see a French home.

44 *"The French are unsanitary."*

The French have a lower living standard than we in the United States. (So do the Poles, the Russians, the Greeks, the Yugoslavs, the Chinese, the

Mexicans, the Hindus, the Turks, and most of the other peoples of the world.)

Sanitary standards rise as the standard of living rises. France is not as prosperous as we are. It is not cheap to install modern plumbing.

45 *"The French don't bathe."*

The French don't bathe often enough. They can't. They don't have real soap. They have had no soap worthy of the name since 1940. The Germans took the soap, for four years. That's a long time.

The ration for Frenchmen today, four months after the war is over, is two cakes of poor ersatz soap per month—20 grams every two months. Most real soap can only be obtained on the black market, where it costs around 125 francs for 310 grams.

46 *"You ride on the subway and the smell almost knocks you out, Garlic, sweat—and perfume!"*

French subways today are overcrowded, hot, untidy, and smell bad. The subways are carrying all the traffic too that used to be carried on buses.

You smell garlic because the French, who are superb cooks, use more of it than we do.

You smell sweat because the French must use a very poor ersatz soap—and don't get enough of that.

You smell perfume because French women would

rather smell of perfume than of an unwashedness which they dislike as much as you do. When you have no soap, perfume comes in mighty handy. In the eighteenth and nineteenth centuries, in the United States as in other countries, perfumes and *eau de cologne* were used to give a pleasant scent where an unpleasant one might otherwise be.

Incidentally, the Chinese will confess to you, if you're a friend, that the scent of white people, no matter how well scrubbed they are, is unpleasant to the Chinese. Body odor is closely related to diet. Change the food people eat and you change the way they smell.

47 *"The French villages are pig-sties. They pile their manure right in front of the houses or in the court-yards."*

Some French villages are pig-sties. Others are not. They do, on the whole, *look* much dirtier than our small towns; they are a lot older, too.

The malodorous custom of piling manure in courtyards or in front of houses is practiced in many villages throughout Europe, including many German villages in south and central Germany (for example, Geislingen, Walldorff, etc.).

48 *"I'd like the French a lot better if they were cleaner."*

That's perfectly understandable.

D. WORK AND LAZINESS

49 *"Why do they knock off work for two to three hours every day?"*

They keep their stores open two to three hours later than we do. (They did when there were things to sell; there's no point in keeping a store open if the shelves are bare.)

The long lunch hour is a custom which is not confined to France. It is found in Italy, Spain, the Balkans and many parts of Germany. It is a custom we find annoying because it interferes with our comfort (as tourists) and because it differs from our way of doing things.

The average Frenchman maintains that a lunch eaten at leisure is a lot better than a chicken-salad-on-toast gobbled down at a drugstore counter. "We take time to live as well as work," one Frenchman said.

The shortage of food, the high cost of restaurant meals, and the fact that only a few factories run messes makes it necessary for the average Frenchman today to go *home* for his lunch.

50 *"The French spend all their time at these cafes. They just sit around drinking instead of working."*

The same people don't sit at the cafes all day. Watch them come and go. They worked before they sat down and they go to work after they leave. Many business negotiations are carried on at a cafe; and many business deals are concluded there.

We Americans don't approve of the cafe custom. We don't approve of a leisurely lunch hour. All this means is that the French custom is different from ours.

The cafe is something we just don't have in the States. It isn't a bar. It isn't a saloon. It's more like a club. It's the place a man can get away from a crowded home. It's the place he can meet his friends. It's the place a man takes his girl or wife and family—to have coffee (when they used to have coffee), beer, wine; to read the papers, play checkers, write letters. To the French, the cafe is a place to relax, not a place to get drunk.

"Café", by the way, means coffee. Before the war most of the drinking at the cafes was coffee drinking. There is no coffee now. Blame the Germans for that.

51 *"They are lazy."*

Some are; some are not. No one works longer hours, works harder or is more thrifty than the French farmer.

On the whole, the French take life and work at a more leisurely, unhurried pace than we do. On the whole, the output of an average French worker is less than that of an average American worker. France has far less industrialization, mechaniza-

38

tion, and labor-saving devices than we do. That is also true of nearly all other nations in the world.

The French claim they get more out of life than we do. They say they have better music, art, poetry, philosophy, literature. They say they take time to enjoy living. They say they do not kill themselves in the endless pursuit of money.

52 *"You can drive all through Paris and never see anyone working."*

It depends on where you drive and where you look. Incidentally, where did you get the gas and time to drive "all through Paris"?

53 *"They're primitive. French farmers still wear wooden shoes."*

The French farmer is more sensible than you think. The French farmer wears wooden shoes because they insulate his feet against mud and damp much better than leather can.

France does not have the very hot summer days and nights we get in the Middle West. The landscape of France is not deforested because for centuries the French have been careful to re-plant the trees they've cut down. And so the rivers of France run deep all year round, and the French soil is cool and moist, and wooden shoes come in mighty handy. The French farmer finds them more practical than leather shoes.

54 *"Why don't the French work their fields? You see farm after farm without anyone working. The French are lazy."*

There were, until very recently, 2,230,000 Frenchmen *in Germany* as PWs, slave labor, deportees.

After World War I, the young people of France streamed from the farms to the cities. In 1930, whole villages in some areas of France were deserted. Farm legislation made an effort to check the flow of population from the country to the cities, but it was not very effective.

It is, however, wrong to deduce from this that the French are "lazy". The French farmer has always been regarded as one of the most industrious and thrifty in the world.

Perhaps another reason that more Frenchmen are not in the fields is that French people have been killed by mines laid by the Germans. In one month this year 150 were killed or maimed in this manner.

E. MORALS

55 *"French women are easy pick-ups."*

The French women who are easy pick-ups are those who are easily picked up.

It is as foolish to generalize about French women from the few any American has met as it would be to generalize about *all* American women from the few a man might pick up near an Army camp.

56 *"French women are immoral."*

Which French women?

Most French girls before the war had far less freedom than our girls back home. A great many were not permitted to go out without a chaperone. France is dominantly Catholic in religion and in morals.

The immoral Frenchwomen are, of course, the easiest women for us to meet. That's why we meet so many of them.

57 *"How do the French themselves feel about all the streetwalkers? How can they close their eyes to all the immorality?"*

They don't close their eyes to it. That's the first difference between French and American attitudes toward prostitution. The French recognize that prostitution exists, and regulate it. Before the war, all prostitutes were inspected regularly, licensed, and had their activities strictly limited to specific areas. The French think that legalized prostitution gives health protection to the general public and that the restriction of prostitution to known areas protects decent women from being molested.

Today there is undoubtedly an abnormal number of prostitutes in France. Many girls who cannot

41

live on their wages take to the street. Thousands of French women have lost their sweethearts, husbands, homes. The same thing is happening all over Europe. It is another of the appalling consequences of the war Germany started.

A Frenchman who took a walk in Paris recently, said to an American friend, "In forty years of living in Paris, I have never seen so many prostitutes! And in respectable neighborhoods! It's disgraceful!"

The French, by the way, are shocked by the rude way in which GIs talk to a woman, and by the number of unpleasant experiences decent French women have had with intoxicated and amorous American soldiers.

58 *"French women are too damned expensive."*

Prices are made by demand and supply. If there weren't so many men after the same commodity, prices would come down.

If you want to see how much it costs a French woman to live, see question § 86.

59 *"The French drink too much."*

The French think we do. You very rarely see a Frenchman drunk. They don't go in for whiskey. They have never liked cocktails. They are a wine-drinking people: they have a right to be—French grapes and wines are among the best in the world.

In 1942, $1,130,000,000 was spent in the U.S. in retail liquor establishments. In 1939, there were 135,934 drinking places doing an annual business of $1,385,032,000. The *Economic Almanac* of 1944–45 states that in 1937, 5.1% of our per capita outlay was spent on alcoholic beverages.

60 *"Every time a French girl sits down she pulls her dress or skirt up."*

She isn't trying to call your attention to her legs. She is trying to save wear and tear on old clothes, or on new clothes which are made of such shoddy material that they won't take much wear.

61 *"The French are immoral. They are morally decayed."*

That is a very broad and vague statement. How can it be proved?

The French, like many other European peoples, are far less Puritanical than we are in their manners, love-making, conversation and conduct. Europeans often say we Americans are a young and "unsophisticated" nation; we retort that they are old and "immoral". Their morality *differs* from ours on certain matters. Whether it is less "moral" or more "uninhibited" depends on your point of view.

Don't judge France by the Montmartre: the Montmartre *caters* to foreign tourists in search of the risqué.

France is a very devout nation. It has a religious Catholic population (only one million Frenchmen are Protestants). The French have a very strong family system, a very low divorce rate, and a much lower crime rate than we do.

From the American point of view, what is more important than anyone's manners or customs are the things he believes in and fights for. In this sense, we agree with the idea of Thomas Jefferson: "Resistance to tyrants is obedience to God."

For over 900 years France has been one of the great civilizations of the world. "Within the framework of the Third Republic . . . there lived and flourished a civilization so brilliant, so human, so gracious and beautiful, that mankind will be in its debt forever . . . When free men look back upon this Republic, they will remember . . . the artists and thinkers, the poets, musicians, and scientists who made France a temple of the Western spirit." *(New York Times.)*

62 *"They kiss right in the open—in the streets."*

This always startles Americans—at first.

Kissing on both cheeks is the traditional French greeting between old friends.

For their love-making, the French prefer privacy, if available—just as we do.

63 *"How can they put up with the custom of having women attendants in the men's rooms?"*

Because it is an old custom and it does not embarrass *them*. If you lived in France long enough, it would probably cease embarrassing you.

F. AUTOMOBILES AND LOCOMOTIVES

64 *"Why do the French drive so g–d– fast?"*

The French ask the same question about the Americans. French traffic has speeded up with the introduction of thousands of American jeeps, command cars, and trucks. It is not generally believed that American jeep and truck drivers are distinguished for their caution or their regard for pedestrians. French drivers are as terrified of our driving as we are indignant about theirs.

65 *"The French drive like lunatics! They don't obey traffic rules; they don't even use common sense."*

Most Frenchmen are probably not as skillful drivers as most Americans.

Their traffic rules and system are inferior to ours.

But foreigners who drive in America are astonished by the speed, daring and recklessness of American driving.

The statistics on automobile accidents and deaths in the United States are nothing for us to be proud of. Even allowing for the greater amount of cars we have and the greater amount of driving we do, our automobile accident rate is the highest in the world

A foreigner in Paris, like a foreigner in New York, might well feel like the farmer who spent most of his vacation in a big city jumping out of the way of cars. "Darn these furriners!" he cried. "They even put spot-lights on their automobiles so's they can find the pedestrians to run down at night!"

66 *"The French can't drive a car. They can't keep it up. They ruin vehicles."*

The French, on the whole, certainly do not drive as well, keep a car up as well, or protect their vehicles as well as we do. Neither do women, compared to men.

We have had more mechanical training, more technical experience. And at the present time we have incomparably better maintenance facilities.

67 *"French railroads are a mess. Their equipment is terrible."*

They are.

46

The state of the French railroads can be traced to these facts: (1) the Nazis took away most of the best French rolling stock; (2) we shot up a good deal of the French railway system before and after D-Day.

After liberation, the French found only 35% of their locomotives, 37% of their freight cars, and 34% of their passenger coaches.

Before the war France had some of the finest trains in the world, and some of the fastest short-distance runs in the world.

As in all European countries, France had three classes of accommodations. Their third-class coaches were less comfortable than ours; but their first-class accommodations were in many respects better than anything we had in America.

68 *"We give them locomotives and they don't even run them."*

Then who does? The locomotives which the French have *are* running.

the French and

69 *"The French aren't our kind of people. The Germans are."*

What makes a nation "our kind of people"? The way they look? The clothes they wear? The kind of plumbing they have? Or the things they believe in—the things they fight for; the things they fight against?

The French believe that all men are born and created equal. They believe in freedom of speech, freedom of religion, freedom of the press, the rights of minorities, government of the people, by the people, and for the people. What do the Germans believe in?

The French were our allies during the American Revolution. They were our allies in 1917–1918. They were our allies in 1941–1945. What were the Germans?

The French proved, by their acts, that they *are* "our kind of people". The Germans proved, by their acts, that they are *not* "our kind of people". Look at the record. It's a record of facts, not assumptions; it's a record of deeds, not pretense.

You can't tell what Germany is really like, because you are not seeing Germany: you are seeing a Germany that has been beaten, conquered, and occupied. You are seeing a Germany that has had the arrogance and insolence knocked out of her. You can't tell what "the Germans" are really like, because you are seeing Germans who are being forced to obey themselves—under military government.

"Forsake not an old friend, for the new is not comparable unto him"—Ecclesiasticus, IX, 10.

70 *"The French are not as clean as the Germans."*

Perhaps not.

If the Germans had had no soap for five years they wouldn't be a clean as they might like to be.

A learned man once said, "An untidy friend is better than an immaculate enemy."

71 *"The Germans are easier to get along with than the French, because the Germans are law-abiding."*

The Germans obey the law—even if the laws are barbaric laws. The Germans obey their leaders—even if their leaders are savage, corrupt and obscene. The Germans obeyed Bismarck; they obeyed Kaiser Wilhelm; they obeyed Hitler.

Would the French have obeyed such men and such policies? Would we Americans?

72 *"The French are not as efficient as the Germans in large scale, mass production."*

The French are not as efficient as the Germans in building tanks, guns, planes, flame-throwers, concentration camps and torture chambers.

The French are not efficient in starting wars. The Germans are. German efficiency is used against peaceful, decent people.

What does "efficiency" really mean? Is it only a matter of output and production charts and impressive statistics? Are the Germans more "efficient" in providing happiness or peace to their people? Are the Germans more "efficient" in building decency, kindness, respect for human life? Has German "efficiency" led to greater wisdom, better art, deeper morals, finer philosophies?

A prison is one of the most "efficient" institutions man ever created—but who wants to live in it?

73 *"The French are trouble-makers; the Germans are really peaceful at heart."*

Who started the war anyway? Who started the "trouble-making"?

The facts prove beyond any shadow of a doubt that the French wanted peace. From 1918 to 1939, they pleaded for peace, argued for peace, built for peace. Their army, their equipment, their fortifications, their entire military strategy was devoted to a war of *defense*.

The Germans invaded France in 1870; the Germans invaded Belgium and France in 1914; the Germans invaded Poland and Czechoslovakia in 1939. Three wars started by the same nation in seventy years. This is strange conduct for a "peaceful" people.

Incidentally, one of the most effective propaganda weapons the Nazis used, from 1933 to 1939, and one which pulled the wool over the eyes of a lot of gullible people, was the constant cry: "We Germans want peace. We will never go to war. Our aims in Europe are satisfied."

The Japs said they wanted peace in 1931—and they invaded Manchuria. The Germans said they wanted peace in 1938—and they grabbed Austria. Mussolini said Italy wanted peace in 1935— and invaded Ethiopia. Germany promised the world peace again in 1938, after the Munich agreement—and then invaded Czechoslovakia.

It's all reminiscent of the story of the two drunks. The first kept beating his friend on the head with a club, wailing all the while: "You're my pal, my buddy, my best friend, and I love you." And the second replied tearfully, "I believe you—but you have such a funny way of showing it."

74 *"We'd be a lot smarter to be allies of the Germans and fight the French."*

What in the world would we fight the French *about*?

What ideas, principles or goals would we have in common with the Germans?

"What boots it at one gate to make defence, and at another to let in the foe?"—John Milton.

75 *"The French aren't industrious, the way the Germans are."*

This is true. Perhaps it would have been a lot better for all of us if the Germans weren't so industrious. It was German industriousness in six short years, 1933–1939, that built the most terrible army, air force, tank force, bombs and submarine warfare the world had ever seen. No one ever accused Al Capone of not being industrious.

76 *"The French have no courage. Why can't they defend themselves against the Germans?"*

Maybe it would be better to ask, "Why don't the Germans pick on someone their own size?"

Modern warfare is not simply a matter of courage. A great lightweight can't lick a great heavyweight—even if he has courage to spare.

Hitler threw the manpower and industrial resources of over 80,000,000 Germans against 40,000,000 Frenchmen. The French did not have, and *could* not have had, the military and industrial power to beat Germany. (For instance, for the past hundred years France has not had enough coal, especially coking coal, to supply her peacetime needs. French iron ore normally flows to Germany's Ruhr valley for smelting, just as the ore of Minnesota goes to the coal and limestone area of Pittsburgh.)

France was beaten by Germany because Germany was enormously superior to France in manpower, equipment, resources, armament, and strategy. Germany had the incalculable advantage of having planned an offensive, Blitzkrieg war— while France, which wanted peace desperately, devoted its energies and training entirely to *defensive* measures. (That's why they built the Maginot Line.) The few advocates of modern mechanized armies (such as General de Gaulle) were like voices crying out in the wilderness. German propaganda, and "fifth column" activities financed from Berlin, helped to demoralize and confuse a nation that didn't want war in the first place.

The French lost 1,115,000 men and women, military and civilian, in dead, wounded and disabled. That is an enormous loss for a nation of 40 million. (The United States military casualties, up to V-J Day, were about 1,060,000 in dead and wounded.)

77 *"The French don't even have enough men to stand up against the Germans."*

True. That, in fact, is one of the things the Germans counted on in 1870, in 1914 and in 1939.

France never fully recovered from the results of World War I. Here is what the French lost from 1914 to 1918:

Killed or died	1,357,800
Wounded	4,266,000
Prisoners and missing	537,000
Total	6,160,800

The French had mobilized 8,410,000 men. They lost 6,160,800 —or 73.3%. No nation had ever suffered such a staggering loss. No nation had shown a greater record of sheer courage and tenacity. There was scarcely a family in France that did not number one or more of its members among the dead. World War I left France weak and exhausted—for the second war Germany launched against her within a generation.

The catastrophic effects of the first World War hit France particularly hard because they were added to the serious problem of a declining birth-rate. By 1939, largely because of the losses of World War I, the proportion of the French population under 20 years of age was small—and growing smaller; the proportion of Frenchmen over 60 years of age was large—and growing larger.

In 1940, after occupation, the Germans tried to cripple France permanently by a policy of deliberate starvation and the segregation of the sexes. The Germans held nearly 2,000,000 French men in German prison and work camps—away from French women. The German policy of malnutrition worked so well that in 1945, when the French government was drafting men to re-create a French army, it was found that 40% of all Frenchmen called up for physical duty were physically unfit. In 1942, at the height of German occupation, there were 500,000 more deaths than births in France.

78 *"The French didn't put up a real fight against the Germans. They just let the Heinies walk in."*

No one—least of all the French themselves—will try to deny the enormity of the defeat and the humiliation France suffered in 1940. French military leadership and strategy was tragically inadequate. But this does not mean that the French did not put up a "real fight".

In the six week Battle of France, from May 10 to June 22, 1940, the French lost, in military personnel alone, 260,000 wounded and 108,000 killed. A total of 368,000 casualties in six weeks is not something to pass off lightly.

Yes, the Germans gave the French a terrible beating. But it took the combined strength of the United States, Great Britain, Soviet Russia, Canada, etc., to beat the Germans. It's asking rather a great deal of France to match such strength against hers. (See question § 76.)

79 *"The French aren't cleaning up their bombed cities. Just compare them to the German cities. In Munich and Stuttgart the Germans got busy and cleaned up their streets."*

The French lack materials, trucks, gasoline, bulldozers and manpower.

The Germans started cleaning up their cities (before we invaded Germany) with PWs—French,

Polish, Russian, etc. The Germans had 2,230,000 able-bodied French men and women inside Germany as PWs, slave laborers, etc.

Today, it is not the Germans alone who are cleaning up their cities. It is our Military Government which supervises reconstruction and assigns German civilians and PWs to the job. Germany is an occupied country; France is not. Apart from these qualifications, the Germans *would* probably do a quicker and better job of cleaning up their cities than the French. So what?

80 *"The French cleaned out Stuttgart, we saw long convoys of stuff going back to France—machinery, goods, cattle, supplies, horses,—long convoys of stuff looted from the Germans."*

Where had the Germans gotten the stuff? From France. The long convoys you saw were not "loot": they were authorized reparations, approved by the United States, Great Britain and Russia. The French had a right, under international law, to take back some of the commodities the Germans had stolen from them.

Here are sample figures on what the Germans took out of France:

Wheat	2,340,000	metric tons
Oats	2,360,000	—
Hay	1,530,000	—
Straw	1,870,000	—

```
Potatoes . . . . . . . . . . . . . . . .600,000   —
Fresh fruits  . . . . . . . . . . . .290,000   —
Cider apples. . . . . . . . . . . . .210,000   —
Sugar  . . . . . . . . . . . . . . . .180,000   —
Horses. . . . . . . . . . . . . . . . .650,000   —
Eggs  . . . . . . . . . . . . . . 150,000,000  dozen
Wine . . . . . . . . . . . . . . 190,000,000  gals
Beer  . . . . . . . . . . . . . . . 83,000,000   —
Champagne  . . . . . . . . . 16,000,000   —
Cognac  . . . . . . . . . . . . . .  3,458,000   —
```
(1 metric ton equals 2,205 pounds, approximately equal to 1 long ton of 2,240 lbs.)

The Germans also "requisitioned" or damaged:

668,253,000,000 Francs worth of agricultural products;

448,474,000,000 Francs worth of industrial and commercial products;

246,361,000,000 Francs worth of war material.

(See also question § 106.)

81 *"The French troops in Germany had the women terrorized."*

The French army, as any other, had to cope with disorderly conduct, looting, rape, and other acts of violence by their soldiers against enemy populations.

If you think French troops misbehaved in Germany, you might ask how German troops behaved in Poland, Russia, Greece, Holland.

If you were a French soldier, whose land had

been invaded, whose wife or sister or mother had been taken into a German concentration camp and raped or killed, you might have found it difficult to control your emotions.

Lastly, a good many French women have been in terror of American troops, especially in Paris. Our MP records testify to a deplorable amount of drunkenness, molesting of women and street fights—by Americans.

82 *"The French soldiers were supposed to hate the Germans, but they didn't waste any time shacking up with German girls."*

That is as deplorable as the same conduct on the part of Americans.

PRICES:

"We're being gypped"

83 *"Fifty francs to a dollar is blackmail! The dollar is worth at least 100–200 francs."*

The rate of 50 francs to the dollar was established in 1942 at the Casablanca conference. France didn't set the rate; the rate was agreed upon by the governments of France and the United States.

Why was the rate set at such a disadvantage to the American dollar?

First, to keep American soldiers from buying up many of the articles which the French themselves desperately needed. The American soldier gets his lodging, food, clothes free—and his PX rations at extremely low prices. The French people do not get their lodging, food, clothes free—and the prices they pay for the things we get at our PXs (if they can even get those things) are very high.

Secondly, the dollar was kept low in order to keep prices from going even higher than they are now.

If the dollar had had more purchasing power in France, American purchasers could have cleaned out the shops of, say, Paris. Prices would be much higher than they already are.

(Incidentally, if the dollar had been pegged at 100 francs, say, the French private would have been getting $8 a month pay, at the wartime pay rate of 800 francs per month. He would now be getting $1.80 *per month* at the peacetime pay rate of 6 francs per day.)

84 *"The high prices and inflation in France are a disgrace."*

Inflation is more than a disgrace—it is a tragedy. The French are hit by it much harder than we are.

The basic reason for inflation, for very high prices, is the great shortage of food and goods and things which people need and have the money to buy. When there is not enough of anything (except money), prices go up. When there is too much, prices go down; when supply and demand operate in a healthy, normal fashion, prices are reasonable.

Inflation in France will end when there are enough goods for all the people who want to buy them. As long as there are severe shortages, prices will be high.

85 *"When we buy nice presents to send home, we pay through the nose!"*

It's the same nose you pay through when you buy nice presents in the States. At home, most of us did not buy luxury articles. Here we do. How often, back home, did you buy fine French perfume for your girl? How much did you pay?

The French government has taken the luxury tax off articles purchased by American soldiers. The French pay it; we don't. Who is paying through the nose?

Prices in France are certainly very high. But high prices hit the French much harder than they hit any of us Most of the things we buy in France are luxuries. A shot of cognac is definitely a luxury for most Frenchmen.

Examine the following prices, which the French are paying—if and when they can get the articles:

July 1945

Bread 1 kg. (2.2 lbs.) . . . . 7.40 francs
Beef 1 kg. . . . . 97.00 —
Butter 1 kg. . . . . 113.00 —
Eggs 1 dz. 45.60 —
Soap 1 kg. 31.00 —
Electricity, 1 kw. . . . . 4.64 —
Gas, m.3 . . . . 3.29 —
Cotton Socks . . . . 150.00 —
(when you can get them)
Undershirt . . . . 350.00 —
(plus 8 points)
Suit. 1,500–1,000 francs
(but try to find one)

The average skilled worker in France gets 1,200–1,300 fr ($24–26) a week. How much cognac, perfume, kerchiefs, bracelets can the average Frenchman buy—after he gets done paying for food and rent? How much can the French GI buy—on pay of 6 cents a day?

87 *"What did the French ever do to make up for the ridiculous exchange rate?"*

The French government has made an effort to reduce the low purchasing power of the American dollar by:

1. Giving each U.S. soldier in France a gift of 850 francs a month (this is over four months pay for a French private);
2. Reducing the cost of gifts purchased at PXs by 9–42%;
3. Making luxury tax rebates of 11–47% on gifts purchased at retail stores and sent home via Red Cross wrapping centers;
4. Giving free conducted tours to Americans all through France;
5. Opening special night clubs and entertainment facilities for American soldiers.

88 *"Giving us 850 francs a month is just a way for the French to get off the hook for all the Lend-Lease stuff we've given them."*

The 850 francs are in no way connected with Lend-Lease. The gift is not to be deducted from the French government debt or commitments under Lend-Lease. It has no reciprocal basis of any kind. It is an outright gift. It will ultimately cost the French around $40,290,000.

89 *"This 850 francs a month gift to us has something fishy about it."*

There's nothing fishy about it.

"All looks yellow to the jaundiced eye"—Alexander Pope.

the Black Market

It is. Most Frenchmen think it is, too. The French newspapers are full of daily criticism of the black market.

Why did the black market arise in France? The basic reason for any black market, in France or in any country at war, is that there is a great shortage of certain goods, which people need.

Why were (and are) there great shortages in France? Largely because during four years of occupation, the Germans stripped France bare, picked her clean as a bone. (In Marseille, the food depot for the whole south of France, the Germans took 60% of the food that was being shipped in.) And when the Germans left they took along everything they could lay their hands on.

There was another important reason for the black market. During four years of occupation, thousands of French men and women who were fugitives from the Gestapo or members of the resistance, had no identification cards and no ration cards. They could only live through false papers. They could only live illegally. They could only live by getting food and supplies—from the black market. So the black market took on a quality which we never had in the United States: it became *patriotic* for many people to patronize the black market. It was one way of continuing to fight German rule, one way of getting supplies with which to carry on resistance. It was a weapon *against* the Germans.

The black market in France is not, as it was in America, a market for relative luxuries (gasoline, whiskey, steaks, butter.) In France, no city family could get enough *food* from the rations doled out by the Germans. From 1941 to the liberation of Paris in 1944, the Parisians were getting between 1,067 and 1,325 calories of food per day. 2,400 calories a day is considered the necessary minimum for adults not engaged in heavy work. (The average consumption in the United States is 3,367 calories daily. Our army ration provides 4,000 to 5,000 calories a day.) Even with black market purchases, most Frenchmen have not had enough to eat for four years. Hence the story of two Frenchmen discussing the black market. One said, "Would you be willing to stop buying anything on the black market for a week?" "Certainly not," was the reply, "Do you want my children to go hungry?"

The black market in France will disappear when there is enough food and supplies in the ordinary stores, in sufficient quantity to be sold at reasonable prices. If the French had more transportation to bring the crops into the cities, the black market would do less business.

The Germans, incidentally, were notorious traders on the black market—for personal profit.

The German authorities did not try to stamp out the black market—because they knew it would increase the bitterness of the French people toward their government and leaders. The Germans used every trick in the bag to disrupt the French economy and demoralize French people.

Lastly, where did the French black market get American cigarettes, soap, candy, chocolate, razor blades, shoes? From American soldiers, who sold them—on the black market.

91 *"Why don't the French use stronger methods to stop the black market?"*

The French people ask that question every day.

It is not our job to appraise the energy or the methods of the French government. It is not in place for Americans to tell the French how to run their affairs. This much, however, can be said: France is pulling herself up by the bootstraps. It's very easy to stand to one side and say, "Pull harder. It's a cinch. Just pull harder."

France is still "punch-drunk", uncertain, demoralized from the war and the effects of the war. It is hard for us to realize the appalling toll which the war took from France. It is hard for us to realize how profoundly the entire economic and political structure of France has been shaken by the events from 1940–1945.

France is tired, hungry, discouraged, poor, weak. The French saw their country defeated. They saw some of their leaders and heroes sell them down the river. They hate all this more than we do. They have to live with it.

No Frenchman will deny the mistakes France

has made, the blows France has suffered, the long and difficult road that France must now take. But the *way* in which France will recover, the way in which the French will meet problems as grave and difficult as any she has ever known, is something which the French people, acting democratically, will decide for themselves.

If there is a moral for the world in all this, it is: don't ever let the Germans or any other Fascist power beat you.

If there is a lesson for Americans, it is: we don't kick a friend when he's down—especially when he was knocked down by our enemy.

92 *"The leaders of the French resistance were behind the black market. They all got rich on it."*

This is the exact argument used by Dr. Gœbbels and the German propaganda machine. The Germans wanted to smash the resistance movement; they constantly smeared the leaders of that movement. Gœbbels kept hammering at the idea that those who resisted German rule were simply criminals.

The French resistance *used* the black market during the four years of German occupation. They had to use it, in order to survive. (See question § 90.)

Since the liberation of France, no group in France has more vigorously fought the black market and demanded that the government stop it than the resistance organizations and the resistance leaders.

93 *"The French haven't done a damn thing to stop pleasure driving by Frenchmen."*

The latest check-up on pleasure driving by the French took place on September 25, 1945 when French MPs stopped hundreds of French military vehicles in the greater Paris area in a surprise check-up for official credentials. All French vehicles were stopped and each driver had to produce papers showing the car was being used for official business. French civilians or military personnel who lacked proper papers were booked for court action.

those French

Soldiers

94 *"It burns me up to see a Frenchman using American uniforms."*

It would burn you up more if they were in German uniforms.

Before we invaded North Africa, in 1942, our government arranged to equip eleven French divisions. Why? Because every French soldier took a place that might have had to be filled by an American.

The 11,000 French soldiers who were killed in action *after* D-Day were entitled to the uniforms in which they died.

Question: Where else could the French have gotten uniforms? From the Germans? France was occupied by the Germans when we were equipping the French Army.

Question: Why didn't the French dye their uniforms, to distinguish them from ours? Because they did not have the dyes. Why didn't we dye the uniforms before turning them over to the French? Because we were using our dyes for more important war production purposes. Why didn't we or the French provide more easily recognized French insignia? That was a mistake.

95 *"The French act as if they won the war single-handed."*

Those who do are damned fools. The French did not win this war single-handed. Neither did we. Neither did the Russians or the British or the Chinese.

If you want to form your own opinion about how much the French did to help win the war, ask yourself these questions: Suppose the French army and navy had joined up with the Germans in 1940 (as Hitler tried to get them to do)? Suppose the French armies which were fighting the Germans or the Italians had been fighting us? Suppose there had been no French underground, no French resistance, no French sabotage of German military production, no French espionage for SHAEF, no French guerrillas behind the German lines, no French Maquis in Central France, no FFI inside France as we fought our way through? How many more American lives do you think we would have lost?

96 *"Why don't French soldiers ever clean their uniforms?"*

The French soldier got only *one* full uniform issued to him. It is impossible for him to draw another; it is almost impossible for him to purchase another.

Cleaning takes three to four weeks in France.

Why don't they use cleaning fluid? Because they don't have cleaning fluid.

Why don't they wash their uniforms? They do— but with a very poor ersatz soap. It is the only soap they can get.

81

The French soldier got paid 800 francs *a month* ($16) until September, 1945, when this sum was cut to 180 francs a month ($3.60). (This cut in pay came at about the time the French government announced it would give every American soldier in France 850 francs a month as a bonus.) The French soldier gets a total pay of about 12 cents a day. How well could you keep up your uniform on 12 cents a day?

97 *"In Paris you see hundreds of young Frenchmen, our age, in civilian clothes. Why aren't they all in the Army?"*

Many of them are, even though they are in civilian clothes. Reason? In most French commands (including the Paris area), enlisted men are permitted to wear civilian clothes when they are on pass or off duty. French officers in all commands are permitted to wear civilian clothes when off duty.

It is also worth remembering that in the 1945 draft, the French had to reject 40% of the men called up as physically unfit for military duty (and the standards used were lower than those used in our army). Why were so many young Frenchmen unfit physically? Because they were underfed by the Germans during the occupation. Because tuberculosis and other diseases spread, during the four years of German occupation. Because of the effects of World War I. (See question § 77.) Because

82

the best French youth were killed, wounded, disabled, or taken as slave laborers into Germany.

98 *"The French are sloppy-looking soldiers. One look at them and you know they're not good fighters."*

You don't tell how an army fights by the way it looks. The Greek soldiers wore funny white skirts—but they licked the pants off the dashingly dressed Italians, and they put up an amazing fight against the might of the Wehrmacht, the Panzers, and the Luftwaffe.

German officers called American GIs "sloppy," "careless," "undisciplined" soldiers—but it was the Germans who got the shellacking.

The army of George Washington often looked like a ragged mob. Their fighting record is another story.

The French under General Le Clerc fought their war from the heart of Africa to Lake Chad and up to North Africa in an astonishing campaign. No one sneered at their uniforms then.

It might be helpful to remember that many French soldiers had been guerrilla fighters (in the FFI, the Maquis, the resistance). They still dress, act and carry themselves like guerrillas.

99 *"Why do French soldiers look so sloppy in their uniforms?"*

Some do; some don't. Check this yourself. Look around.

100 *"What got my goat was all the publicity the French soldiers got! Take the Maquis and the FFI—the part they played in the war was exaggerated in the press."*

Local papers always play up local news. Local papers are proud of the deeds of local boys. It was as natural for the French to praise the fighting of the French as it was for the Botsford *Bugel* to give front-page space to the return of Pfc Elmer Glutz on the day we dropped the atomic bomb on Japan.

If it's publicity in the American press which you're objecting to, then criticize American news judgment, not French vanity. The story of the Maquis and FFI was a "natural" news story. It's the kind of story that has hit the front pages ever since there were wars—and newspapers to report on them.

As for the role the FFI and the Maquis played in the fight against Germany, see the statements of General Patton and General Patch, under question § 77.

101 *"The French soldiers stole everything they could get their hands on. They stole our gas, jeeps, trucks, rations. We had to post guards over every vehicle."*

Some French soldiers certainly did steal. We didn't like it.

So did some Americans. The French didn't like that. The French had no monopoly on "moonlight requisitioning"—as any GI knows.

It is worth remembering that the French armies had a very large number of men who had been trained in underground fighting, in guerrilla warfare, in the methods of sabotage and the resistance. Such soldiers live off the land. They're taught to. They're trained to. Our own parachute troops also used "unorthodox methods".

French Collaboration

102 *"The French were all collaborationists."*

That's the line Gœbbels used. The Germans exerted every propaganda effort to make us think there was no real resistance in France. Nazi censorship and Nazi firing squads tried to stop our hearing about the resistance.

For the *facts*, see questions § 17, 18, 104.

103 *"The French mostly collaborated with the Germans."*

The Germans would disagree with that. The Germans tried for four years to get more Frenchmen to collaborate. That's why they killed so many hostages. That's why they destroyed 344 communities for "crimes" not connected with military operations.

The Germans overran France in 1940. For two years they used every promise, trick and pressure to induce the French people to work in Germany for the German war machine. They offered workers better food, clothes, privileges and protection denied them in France under occupation rules. And in all of France, during that entire period, about 75,000 French workers enlisted. The Germans admitted the campaign was a failure.

The LVF (Legion Volontaire Francaise), the French volunteer army that the Germans tried to organize, was a gigantic flop.

For the facts on how the French fought the Germans from 1940 until the liberation, see questions § 17, 18, 104.

104 *"After France fell, the French laid down and let the Germans walk all over them. They just waited for us to liberate them. Why didn't they put up a fight?"*

Millions of French men, women and children put up a fight that took immense guts, skill and patience.

The Fighting French never stopped fighting—in the RAF, North Africa, Italy, and up through France with the U.S. 7th Army.

Here is how the French people inside France fought the Germans after the fall of France:

They sabotaged production in war plants. They destroyed parts, damaged machinery, slowed down production, changed blue-prints.

They dynamited power plants, warehouses, transmission lines. They wrecked trains. They destroyed bridges. They damaged locomotives.

They organized armed groups which fought the German police, the Gestapo, the Vichy militia.

They executed French collaborationists.

They acted as a great spy army for SHAEF in London. They transmitted as many as 300 reports a day to SHAEF on German troops' movements, military installations, and the nature and movement of military supplies.

They got samples of new German weapons and explosive powder to London.

They ran an elaborate "underground railway" for getting shot-down American and British flyers back to England. They hid, clothed, fed and smuggled out of France over 4,000 American airmen and parachutists. (Getting food and clothes isn't easy when you're on a starvation ration yourself. It's risky to forge identification papers.) Every American airman rescued meant half a dozen French lives were risked. On an average, one Frenchman was shot *every two hours*, from 1940 to 1944 by the Germans in an effort to stop French sabotage and assistance to the Allies.

The Germans destroyed 344 communities (62 completely) for "crimes" not connected with military operations. Perhaps the Germans realized better than we do the relentless fight against them which the French people waged.

An official German report, quoted in the *Christian Science Monitor* on December 26, 1942, stated sadly: "For systematic inefficiency and criminal carelessness they (the French) are unsurpassed in the history of modern industrial labor."

"they got off pretty easy in this war"

105 *"Yon wouldn't think they'd even been in the war the way a city like Paris looks."*

No, you wouldn't. You can't tell what the war cost France by a stroll down the Champs Elysees, just as you couldn't tell what the war cost America by a walk down the Atlantic City boardwalk.

You can't, in Paris, see the 1,115,000 French men and women and children who died, were wounded, were in concentration camps, or were shot as hostages. You can't see the food and supplies that were taken from France. You can't see the 12,551,039,000 man-hours of labor that the Germans took for themselves. You can't see the meagre rations that the French were fed. You can't see the malnutrition that the Germans caused. (70% of the men and 55% of the women in France lost an average of 12% of their weight.)

You can't see the increase (300–400%) in tuberculosis, diphtheria, typhoid fever, infantile paralysis. You can't see the number of babies who were born dead because of the food and milk shortages. You don't see rickets on the Champs Elysees.

If you want more facts, read the answer to the next question.

106 *"French got off pretty easy in the war."*

What do you call "pretty easy"? Here is what the war cost France!

In people

Military casualties:

Killed	200,000
Wounded	230,000
Total	430,000

Civilian casualties:

Killed in bombings	60,000
Killed in Battle of France 1940	30,000
Killed in other military operations	20,000
Shot or massacred in France	40,000
Total civilians *killed* in France	150,000

Deportees killed or died in Germany:

Political prisoners	130,000
Laborers	20,000
Prisoners of War	30,000
Total	180,000

Total civilians and deportees killed or died . . 320,000

Disabled civilians:

In France	127,000
Deportees (returned from Germany)	228,000
Total	335,000

Total military and civilian killed 530,000
Total military and civilians killed,
  wounded, disabled 1,115,000

In materials
1,785,000 buildings were destroyed.

5,000 bridges were blown up.

Three-fifths of all French railroad stock was either destroyed or taken to Germany by Germans as they retreated in 1945.

Half of all the livestock in France was lost or stolen.

Three-fourths of all the agricultural equipment was lost.

12,500,000,000 man-hours of labor, which millions of Frenchmen were forced to perform for the Germans, were lost to France.

The national debt *increased* 32 billion dollars.

These figures represent a loss to France of half of her national wealth—or the total earnings of all Frenchmen, for two years.

IN LABOR

Deportees	765,000
Forced workers in France	850,000
Industrial workers in French plants (working for Germany)	2,500,000
Agricultural workers growing crops for German conscription	780,000
Total	4,895,000

Hours of work lost to France due to mass deportations	7,427,304,000
Hours of work lost to France because of forced labor in France for the Germans	5,124,335,000
Total	12,551,639,000

IN MONEY

Destruction of buildings, agriculture,
industry, war material etc. 2,342,000,000,000

German exchange extortion (setting
the franc at 20 francs to the mark,
instead of at the real value 10
francs to the mark.) 1,832,000,000,000

Pensions to military and civilian
dead and disabled 359,000,000

Cash payments to maintain German
army of occupation. 2,353,480,000,000

Agricultural products taken by
Germans or damaged 668,253,000,000

Transport and Communication
damaged. 1,527,222,000,000

Industry and Commerce requisitioned
or damaged. 448,474,000,000

Clearing and removal costs 556,580,000,000

War material taken by Germans or
damaged. .246,361,000,000

Special charges imposed on France
in addition to the direct costs of
German occupation 102,000,000,000

Estimated total money cost to France of the
war: 98 billion dollars.

Estimated total cost to U.S.—300 billion dollars.

France is about one fourteenth the size of the
United States.

You can put nearly all of France into Utah and
Nevada.

107 *"Why don't they get to work and rebuild their country?"*

The French Minister of Finance recently reported that France's industries are beginning to operate at 70% of capacity. The rebuilding of France is a tremendous job which will take a long time. Shortages of coal, gasoline, electricity, power, transport, and manpower have made a more rapid recovery impossible.

In 1944, after liberation, France found that of its pre-war transportation, the following were left:

35% of the locomotives,
37% of the freight cars,
38% of the trucks and automobiles,
33% of the merchant marine.

The most important single factor which is holding up French production is the shortage of coal. On February 3, 1945, our Office of War Information analyzed economic conditions in France and pointed out how the coal crisis has plunged France into a vicious circle. Mines could not operate without timber pit props to shore up the ceilings of tunnels in coal veins as they were expanded. But the transportation needed to bring in the timber also needed coal with which to operate.

Coal shortages have caused as many shut-downs of French factories as have the grave shortages of other essential raw materials.

And never forget the loss to France of 1,115,000

people (killed, wounded or disabled) out of a population estimated at around forty million in 1940. This is a staggering blow to the manpower needed for rebuilding.

French

Politics

108 *"All French politicians are corrupt."*

That's as silly as saying that all American politicians get graft. Some French politicians are corrupt. So are some American politicians.

Incidentally, the German propaganda line for French politics was, "All French politicians are corrupt." The Germans wanted the French people to lose confidence in their leaders, in their government, and—most of all—in democracy itself. The Germans ran a gigantic smear campaign before the war, during the war, and during the occupation. The only French politicians of importance whom the Germans did *not* smear were—Petain and Laval. They, said the Nazis, were not corrupt. Odd, isn't it?

109 *"The French don't have a decent political system. They've got too many parties. They never get together."*

The French political system is a democracy. It is like ours in its basic principles: freedom of speech, freedom of religion, freedom of the press, freedom of the vote, minority rights, protection under the law, trial by jury, etc.

The system differs from ours as far as parties are concerned: we have a "two-party" form of administration; the French have many parties.

The French have a political party for almost every conceivable political position. They don't believe that "there are two ways of looking at things"; the French think there are dozens of ways, and that if enough people hold to any one way they have a right to be represented in the government.

French electoral practice has not encouraged party organization such as ours. The elections to the Chamber of Deputies are more like our municipal (city) elections than our national elections. In our city elections, people frequently vote for their friends and neighbors,—for men rather than parties. This is true in France, too.

The French multiple-party system has this advantage: it gives every group of any size a voice in government, a chance to get its program considered, a chance to get certain laws passed.

The multiple-party system has this grave disadvantage: in France, no one party controls a majority of the votes in the Chamber of Deputies. Cabinets are always combination or coalition cabinets. The Premier has to rely on persuasion. It is easy for such cabinets to be overthrown. It is relatively hard for such cabinets to work together, on a common program, for many years; with each new problem or each new crisis, the cabinet can easily be broken up.

The French today are very much aware of the dangers and disadvantages of a multiple-party system. How they will solve it, how they will translate wide representation into simpler administration is their problem. They are trying to solve it—democratically.

Don't be fooled by the names of the French parties. The Radical Socialist party, for example, is neither radical nor socialist. It is the party of small farmers and the lower middle-class; it is a middle-of-the-road party. (Its name is a carry-over from the past.)

For the past twenty years, the great majority of Frenchmen have voted for men and parties that were neither extreme Left nor extreme Right.

In the last pre-war elections of 1936, the parties of the Popular Front (Radical Socialist, Socialist, and Communist), which stood for a sort of New Deal program, got 382 seats in the Chamber of Deputies out of a total of 608. The parties of the Right, which opposed the Popular Front, got 222 seats.

Since the liberation, the French have held municipal elections in May 1945 and cantonal elections in September 1945. The voting strength of the main parties in those elections was approximately as follows:

Name of Party	% vote cast May 1945	% vote cast Sept. 1945
Communist Party	17	21
Socialist Party	15	24
Radical Socialist Party	32	24
Popular Republican Movement	5	9

111 *"The French are Communist."*

The Communist Party got 10 seats hi the Chamber of Deputies in the 1932 elections, and 72 out of 608 seats in the 1936 elections. For their vote in 1945, see question § 110.

112 *"France is a decadent nation."*

How does one measure decadence?
The Germans said, "Democracies are decadent."